Don't Fight the Process

Yielding totally to God's plan to make you great

Archbishop Nicholas Duncan-Williams

Don't Fight the Process
Yielding totally to God's plan to make you great

ISBN: 9781948233033
Copyright ©2018 Nicolas Duncan-Williams

All rights reserved solely by the author. The author guarantees all contents are original and do not infringe upon the legal rights of any other person or work. No part of this book may be reproduced, shared in a retrieval system, or transmitted in any form or by any means, electronic, mechanical, photocopying, and recording, without prior written permission of the Author/Publisher.

Edited and Reprinted in 2020 by:
GOSHEN PUBLISHERS LLC
P.O. Box 1562
Stephens City, Virginia, USA
www.GoshenPublishers.com

Cover Design by:
GOSHEN PUBLISHERS LLC

10 9 8 7 6 5 4 3 2

"Rest in the LORD, and wait patiently for him: fret not thyself because of him who prospereth in his way, because of the man who bringeth wicked devices to pass. Cease from anger, and forsake wrath: fret not thyself in any wise to do evil. For evildoers shall be cut off: but those that wait upon the LORD, they shall inherit the earth."
Psalm 37:7-9

Table of Contents

INTRODUCTION vi

Chapter 1: Process is Inevitable 1
   Life Itself is a Process 2
      The Human Being 2
      The Case of the Butterfly 3
      Plant Life is a Process 4
   No Shortcuts to a Process 4

Chapter 2: Process Sets the Success Stage 9
   God Set the Stage for His Servants 9
   God Set the Stage for Jesus 10
      Jesus Came in His Time 12
      Jesus Took Time to Grow 13
      Jesus' Glorification went through a Process 14
   God Set the Stage for your Success 16

Chapter 3: Process Produces Discipline 19
   Joseph, Preserver of a Nation 19
   Change your Garment 23

Chapter 4: Process Builds Capacity 25
   Time to be Anointed 25
   Time to Learn to be King 27
   Learning to Love and Honor God 28
   The Navy Seals Experience 30

Chapter 5: Process Refines You 33
   From Fishermen to Fishers of Men 33
   Unlearned, Raw, Fishermen 35
   Transformed into World Changers 37
   Process Yields Value 38

Chapter 6: Process Guarantees God Encounters 41
   Knowing God in the Process 41
   Moses Encounters the God of Power 41
   David Encounters the God Worthy of all Worship 44
   Daniel Encounters the God of Wisdom and Supremacy ... 48
   Peter Encounters the God of Immaculate Nature 50
   Paul Encounters the God of Great Salvation 52

Chapter 7: Process Produces Faith and Stability 55
   Faith does not Replace the Process 55
   Job's Faith through Process 56
   God has Set the Limits to your Process 58
   Withstanding the Winds and the Floods 60

- Chapter 8: Process – Clay in the Potter's Hand 65
  - Jeremiah at the Potter 66
  - You are Clay in the Potter's Hand 67
    - Step 1: Selecting the Clay 68
    - Step 2: Mixing the Clay 70
    - Step 3: Forming the Clay 71
    - Step 4: Cutting and Shaping the Clay................................72
    - Step 5: Raising the Temperature.......................................73
- Chapter 9: Process Realities..77
  - Process Requires Christian Character 77
    - Patience – Waiting until it Happens 77
    - Longsuffering 79
    - Self-Control..79
    - Humility..81
  - Process Demands Submission..84
  - Process Takes Time 86
- Chapter 10: Don't Walk in the Spirit of Absalom..........................89
  - Who is your Father? 89
  - Absalom was a Rebellious Child..93
  - The Spirit of Absalom 94
  - Avoid these Killers 98
- Chapter 11: Don't Fight the Process 101
  - Embracing Every Bit of the Process 101
  - Jesus Christ did not Fight the Process 103
  - Discipleship [Mentoring] is Critical... 104
  - Elijah and Elisha 106
  - Learn to Grow under Authority.. 107
  - Check your Motives 109
  - Guard against Competition.. 110
- Chapter 12: Wrestle for the Future 113
  - There is a Blessing in the Tussle... 114
  - Redefine Yourself 115
  - Focus on what is being Changed in You 116
  - Don't be Mindful of Man's Labeling.. 117
- Conclusion... 118

INTRODUCTION

We live in a world where process is often intentionally avoided. Not many people want to go through the process required to achieve or attain any heights. We are a generation of instant coffee, instant worship, instant preaching, instant praise, etc. Even growing a church is placed in the category of the "instants".

Some Pastors want to establish a church and have a membership of 500 in three months. The ministry of the church to produce healthy individuals is no longer a process for many. Service time, for example, is calculated to the last second, and anything beyond the time calculated is considered unacceptable. They call it the spirit of excellence, and God is required to work within the timeframe men have set for Him during church services. It is true, for example, that we cannot have church the whole of Sunday.

We have also moved to another extreme where we do not have ample time for God anymore. We time God the Father. We time the Holy Ghost. We time the operation of God's ministry to us. We tell God to give us the blessing on our terms and after that the show is over. We have forgotten or ignored the truth that God does not perform. He, instead, instructs and commands, and we must be eager to hear Him at all times.

Most people do not like process. They want things immediately. Sometimes the spirit of envy and covetousness makes people want what others have, without going through the process to acquire it.

There are some who see me and think I have prospered. I know some of those people desire what they think I have, instantly. If you read my book, *Providence and Destiny*, you will learn the process that I had to undergo to reach this level. I am still in a process to the next level that God is calling me. Everyone who persevered is someone who endured a process. This book is important because it will help you understand process.

If you do not go through a process, you cannot maintain whatever you get. If you cannot maintain it, you did not earn it. It is not yours. I have lost many things in life, but the things I have kept are those I went through the process to obtain. Those who take shortcuts cut their lives short. Do not look for an easy way out. There isn't one.

If a baby comes out after labor and says "Momma, Momma, I am glad to see you" or "Doctor, you did a good job", the doctor will run because that is impossible. Babies cannot talk the day they are born, nor walk and run the day after. Those are processes of life.

If you avoid the process you will have repetitive cycles. If you want success you must permit a process. If you violate the rules to win a race, you will be disqualified. Paul said, "But I keep under my body, and bring it into subjection: lest that by any means, when I have preached to others, I myself should be a castaway" (1 Cor 9:27). I bring my body under subjection because this body is stubborn and rebellious.

You can have a dream or vision but if you do not subject that dream to process it will die prematurely. The rules of engagement will expose you to some battles you do not want to fight. There are some dreams and visions for which you will need to exercise your spiritual muscle and develop the necessary capability; else, the exposure to those dreams could kill you. Many people died prematurely and are in the cemetery today because they would not subject their dreams to process.

I wrote this book because I see a need for Christians to understand process and, thereby, commit to it. People who fight process will always react to situations. When you have completed a process, you will have the knowledge and discipline to respond responsibly instead of always reacting.

Whenever you react, you are not in control. You are merely responding haphazardly to a situation. When you act, you respond intelligently, and you will generate and develop the muscle to stay at the top. I pray that you will accept and go through the process that God has ordained for you to develop the capacity and stamina for what the future holds, and know that God is with you through the process.

CHAPTER 1: PROCESS IS INEVITABLE

Think of process as a series of actions or steps taken in order to achieve a particular end[1]. God is a God of process. He could have created everything in one day, but because He is a God of process, He created the world in six days (Exo 20:11). Remember that God has the power to do anything. He had the power to create everything all at once; yet, He chose to create through a process and wait patiently for His creation to produce one day at a time.

Process is a necessity! Avoiding the process results in your never attaining the height that God has ordained for you. Subsequently, you will never receive the rewards associated with that height.

God created process to bring you into maturity (1 Cor 13:11). Without that maturity you will mishandle and exploit money, power, opportunities, and yourself. Only through it will you attain and appreciate the things God has in store for you. Without it you have no regard for

---

[1] Lexico. Powered by Oxford. Retrieved July 2019 from www.lexico.com/en/definition/process

people, and dishonor and abuse become the order of your day.

LIFE ITSELF IS A PROCESS

The Human Being

When a woman is pregnant, she has to complete a process to give birth. She has to endure discomfort, body changes, and dietary restrictions to deliver a healthy child.

When a child is born, he or she undergoes a process to learn to speak. Before nine months, babies are attentive to sounds and start babbling. If a baby starts talking straight out of the mother's womb and says, "Mommy, I am hungry", or, "Good job, doctor", it is not natural. The doctor will run off as well as everyone else in the room. Language development follows a pattern, saying a few words at the start until learning to speak properly.

The child learns to crawl, then to lift himself to stand, and then takes first steps, all before perfecting walking. In later stages of development, the child learns to run.

The growing individual goes through several stages: childhood, teenage, adulthood, and then the mature years. We all know that no matter how much you pray for your child, he cannot marry at age six. If your child must marry, he must go through the process of maturation. He must attain physical maturity, spiritual maturity, emotional stability, and a certain level of social status before he can marry. That is a process.

The Case of the Butterfly

Science teaches us that the butterfly goes through four stages of metamorphosis: (1) egg; (2) larva / caterpillar; (3) pupa / a resting stage; and (4) adult. Then, the beautiful, flying adult emerges. All four stages are essential for it to function as a butterfly.

I am sure you know the story of a man who wanted to help a butterfly get out of its pupa stage. He succeeded in "helping" the insect expedite the process. The full pupa stage was not completed. The adult managed to form, but it could not fly like it was intended. That is what happens when you interrupt the process.

Plant Life is a Process

God designed that even plant life should entail a process. If you talk with a farmer, you will learn that the fruit he just handed you resulted from a process.

He first planted the seed in the ground and had to wait for three days. No matter what the farmer does, he may fast and pray without eating or drinking for days; yet, by God's order, seeds must take at least three days to germinate.

Then follows the phase of vegetative growth into branches and leaves before the plant flowers. When flowering begins, the farmer knows he is closer to harvest, but he must pray that all the flowers develop into fruit, and further wait for the fruit to mature for harvest. Life is a process!

No Shortcuts to a Process

A shortcut is an alternative route or an accelerated way of doing or achieving something that is shorter than the one usually taken. There are no shortcuts to a process. If the doctor prescribes you medication, you must consume the full dosage to achieve the complete effect of the prescription. You cannot take all the tablets at once and expect to get well. You also cannot stop taking tablets three days from the start if the doctor says you should take the medication for two weeks.

> **Process is a step-by-step phenomenon by which God, our heavenly Father, sets the total stage for you to grow. He orchestrates events to address all the rough edges of your life until He gets you to look like what He intended and, thereby, build the capacity to function in His calling and purpose for your life.**

One tragedy I have observed for the several years I have been in ministry is that many people are trying to attain new heights without the capacity to do so. It is primarily because they are circumventing the process. They are attempting to run when they have not mastered crawling or standing steadily. They are moving at a pace much faster than their capacity will support. You know the result: they burn out, get tired prematurely, become frustrated, and, subsequently, start veering off their original track. This is why we should not put babes in leadership positions (1 Tim 3:16).

Process is necessary for you to develop the capacity to use your gifts, skills, intelligence, and anointing to run the race that God has ordained for your life. Shortcuts can lead to disasters. If you want to destroy someone, just give him an opportunity for which he or she is not yet ready. If it is before their time, they will destroy themselves. Shortcuts, accelerated routes, and hastiness can have devastating results, especially the following:

1. Shortcuts can lead to *poverty*:
   "The thoughts of the diligent tend only to plenteousness; but of every one that is hasty only to want" *(Pro 21:5); and*
2. Shortcuts can lead to error:
   "Also, that the soul be without knowledge, it is not good; and he that hasteth with his feet sinneth" (Pro 19:2).

Worries, pressures, fears, impatience, and wrong motives can drive you to take shortcuts or adopt ways that circumvent God's processing. As you read this book, take a moment to break every from ungodly pressure and fear.

Bishop Benson Idahosa of blessed memory opened doors for me to preach in America. He told me to keep the anointing against the African demons back, because the demons in America were sophisticated. I did not listen, and it did not work out well. I had not been through the process, so I did not appreciate his instruction and direction.

> "My brethren, count it all joy when ye fall into divers temptations; Knowing this, that the trying of your faith worketh patience. But let patience have her perfect work, that ye may be perfect and entire, wanting nothing."
> (Jam 1:2-4)

As I reflect over those experiences, I understand better that a process is inevitable. No man can bypass the process and expect to achieve the full results of his efforts.

Chapter 2: Process Sets the Success Stage

God Set the Stage for His Servants

The story of the creation of the world and the early beginnings of human life on earth teaches us profound truths about the ways of God (Gen 1:1 – 2:3). Let me reiterate what I said earlier about God as a God of process. Why did He use six days to create the world when He could have done it in a day? He was actually setting the stage for man.

Note also that man was created after everything else was created. God made sure that the stage was set for man before He created him. That was God's way of ensuring that man would be able to fulfill the purpose He had for him. Everything had to be good before He created man.

> **The great lesson here is that God always sets the stage for every important thing He wants to do. Setting the stage is not a one-day, nor a one-year event. Some stages take several years to be fully set.**

GOD SET THE STAGE FOR JESUS

The example of God setting the stage is clear in the redemption of man. Genesis records the event of the sin of Adam and Eve (3:1-24). If you follow the story, you will recognize that discussion ended with a profound statement from God: "And I will put enmity between thee and the woman, and between thy seed and her seed; it shall bruise thy head, and thou shalt bruise his heel" (Gen 3:15).

To clarify the point I want to make here concerning setting the stage, fast forward to the New Testament to see what the Apostle Paul wrote concerning our redemption. To the church in Galatia:

> "Now I say, that the heir, as long as he is a child, differeth nothing from a servant, though he be lord of all; But is under tutors and governors until the time appointed of the father. Even so we, when we were children, were in bondage under the elements of the world: But when the fullness of the time was come, God sent forth his Son, made of a woman, made under the law, to redeem

them that were under the law, that we might receive the adoption of sons." (Gal 4:1-5)

Several generations span from Genesis 3 to Galatians 4. Bible scholars are divided on exactly how much time but, at a minimum, it exceeds 5,000 years. Now, you must understand that these are not years in a vacuum. God did so many things to prepare the whole world for the coming of the Messiah and what He was coming to do:

1. Think of the call of Abraham from his hometown to a land that "I will show you", through Isaac, Jacob, and his twelve sons; through Joseph being sold to Egypt and later becoming prime minister (Gen 2:1).
2. Consider the time in history when a Pharaoh came who did not know Joseph and the persecution and slavery that ensued until God called Moses (Exo 1:8).
3. Think of the ten plagues that came upon the Egyptians to demonstrate God's supremacy over all other gods. Consider particularly the night of the Passover where they had to paint the doorposts with the blood of the Passover lamb to escape death of the firstborn (Exo 7-12).
4. Think through the time of the prophets and what each of them stood for until the time of John the Baptist, and until Jesus was finally born. That must be a long process and God waited until the fullness of time!

Jesus Came in His Time

Why did God not let Jesus come in Genesis soon after Adam sinned? Could He have done that? Yes, He could have. God chose, instead, a process. God Himself watched the years and the generations pass and the events unfold. God was patient to wait until the fullness of the time before sending His Son into our existence.

Think of the many prophecies God had to make through prophet after prophet while He waited for the fullness of the time. The one that was critical concerning the immaculate birth of Jesus Christ was in Isaiah: "Therefore the Lord himself shall give you a sign; Behold, a virgin shall conceive, and bear a son, and shall call his name Immanuel" (Isa 7:14).

Remember, this was said 700 years before Jesus was born. That was process and God Himself had to wait for its completion. In all of these, God was setting the stage.

> **God so perfectly set the stage for Jesus' coming that those of us living in the current dispensation have little difficulty accepting Jesus as the Messiah, and as God Himself. That is the power of process.**

Many people have difficulty doing away with the gospel of Jesus Christ because Jewish history stands as a huge, immovable, indestructible, monument, pointing to Jesus as Messiah and Savior of the world!

Jesus Took Time to Grow

Even His humanity was a process because the immortal does not die. He had to take on human form and that took a process. God had to look for a virgin so Jesus would be unique, different from all fallen humanity and, yes, Mary had to carry Jesus in her womb like any other woman did before her. That was process!

St. Luke made a profound statement about Jesus: "And Jesus increased in wisdom and stature, and in favour with God and man" (Luke 2:52). Think about it, the omniscient and sovereign God took on human form and had to increase in wisdom and stature. That required a process. But the process gave Him favour before God and man. He had to learn the ways of a Jew and subject Himself to Jewish traditions, including going through baptism to be accepted and listened to in His community.

Jesus' Glorification went through a Process

Concerning Jesus' glorification, read what the writer of Hebrews said:

> "So also Christ glorified not himself to be made an high priest; but he that said unto him, Thou art my Son, today have I begotten thee. As he saith also in another place, Thou art a priest for ever after the order of Melchisedec. Who in the days of his flesh, when he had offered up prayers and supplications with strong crying and tears unto him that was able to save him from death, and was heard in that he feared; Though he were a Son, yet learned he obedience by the things which he suffered; And being made perfect, he became the author of eternal salvation unto all them that obey him; Called of God an high priest after the order of Melchisedec." (Heb 5:1-6)

So, you see, Jesus subjected Himself to the process to become the Captain of our Salvation. Jesus kept His eyes and heart focused on the future, on what lay ahead. He maintained the joy of the outcome and that gave Him daily strength to endure all things. We are expected to learn from His example.

> *"Looking unto Jesus the author and finisher of our faith; who for the joy that was set before him endured the cross, despising the shame, and is set down at the right hand of the throne of God." (Heb 12:2)*

Be diligent and guard your heart. Filter every input through the Word of God and God's prophetic intentions for your life. Keep your perspective and be single-mindedly focused on your purpose and assignment.

> *"The light of the body is the eye: therefore when thine eye is single, thy whole body also is full of light; but when thine eye is evil, thy body also is full of darkness. Take heed therefore that the light which is in thee be not darkness." (Luke 11:34-35)*

Flood your mind, filter your hearing, focus your eye, feed your heart, and be filled with light. Be illuminated with the revelation of God's thoughts and plans for you. Seek the mind of God for your future. The mind of God for you is nothing short of goodness, of blessing, of fruitfulness and prosperity. This He affirmed in the words of His prophet Jeremiah:

> *"For I know the thoughts that I think toward you, saith the LORD, thoughts of peace, and not of evil, to give you an expected end. Then shall ye call upon me, and ye shall go and pray unto me, and I will hearken unto you. And ye shall seek me, and find me, when ye shall search for me with all your heart. And I will be found of you, saith the LORD: and I will turn away your captivity, and I will gather you from all the nations, and from all the places whither I have driven you, saith the LORD; and I will bring you again into the place whence I caused you to be carried away captive." (Jer 29:11-14)*

God Set the Stage for your Success

God uses the principle of a process to set the stage for everything, including your life. He can see 25 years of your life from now. God has set a stage for you. He wants you undergo a process to enable you function within the stage He has set. That means if you skip the process, you operate outside your predetermined stage.

Within that stage, He has programmed every activity and event in accordance with what He intends to do at any time in your life. This calls for you to perfectly fit into God's plan. If you avoid the process, you will miss the opportunities God has planted at the key milestones of your life.

> **It is a tragedy for you to operate outside the stage God has set for your success. The result is unnecessary troubles, confusion, extreme suffering not according to the will of God, and eventual failure.**

You have the option of going through the process so you will walk in the stage God has set for every good thing He has for you in your future. If God did not set the stage, you would have a merry-go-round experience, not discovering His path for your life. I believe you are a wise person so you will go through the process like Jesus did!

God makes all things beautiful in His time. When God's time has not come for anything He promised you, it just means you are not at the stage for that thing to happen. Within the stage, favor goes ahead of you, and doors are opened before you get there. God will not entrust anything to someone who is not ready to be a good steward over it.

> "Think of the stage as the fertile grounds God prepares for your seed to grow and mature into a tree that bears fruit in its season. Being confident of this very thing, that he which hath begun a good work in you will perform it until the day of Jesus Christ." (Phi 1:6)

Let God be true and every man a liar!

Chapter 3: Process Produces Discipline

The story of Joseph is familiar to all good students of the Bible. His story stands out as exemplary discipline through a process (Gen 37-47).

If you follow the story, you understand that between the time God gave Joseph the dreams and their fulfillment, was considerable. Fulfillment of God's promises and purposes do not happen overnight, nor do they come on a silver platter. Joseph had to persevere through the process.

By the time he reached high rank, which was the fulfillment of the dreams, he had developed the discipline required to flourish at that level. That explains how he was able to manage success in a strange land.

Joseph, Preserver of a Nation

During his teenage years, he was the envy of his brothers; yet, he still walked in obedience. That established his father's fondness of him, and instigated his process.

He was thrown into a pit, the lowest and darkest place one could ever find himself, a place of no return.

Everything was shattered and there was no hope. As a slave in Potiphar's house, he had no personal rights and was wrongfully imprisoned. When he became Prime minister, he had to face his brothers who had sold him into slavery. We can learn truths of process from Joseph:

1. When you are thrown into the darkest places in life, whether for any mistakes you made or from envy of the people around you, you have an opportunity to trust and hope in the God who spoke to you and made promises to you. He only can get you out according to His timetable for your life.
2. What do you do when you are taken from family, friends, and loved ones, into a strange land? You can complain or depend on God and keep your faith in Him intact.
3. When you go through a situation like Joseph did, languishing in prison unjustly, the tendency may be to seek revenge. Joseph did not retaliate. He controlled his emotions. That is discipline.
4. It takes discipline to learn to take orders, especially if you are a slave. From his story, it is evident that Joseph followed instructions while living under authority in Potiphar's house. He was obedient there just as he had been in his father's house.

> **You cannot command unless you have been commanded. You cannot teach unless you have been taught. You cannot be in authority unless you have been under authority. It is all a process and requires discipline and self-control.**

Joseph was rising in the ranks and had oversight of Potiphar's money. He was trustworthy: he never stole from Potiphar; he never forged documents; and he did not scheme with other servants to deceive their master. Potiphar prospered because of Joseph.

The peak of a disciplined life was when Potiphar's wife tempted Joseph. It happened repeatedly. Day after day, Joseph consistently demonstrated that he could rule over the amorous passions that arouse in every man, especially when a woman is seducing him. This is where many men usually fall. Joseph showed utmost discipline.

The people you expect to remember you in critical moments may forget you, but that is not an opportunity to lose guard, be angry and bitter, and rage. The God you serve never forgets you. If it seems He is not coming through, simply know that He is setting the stage for your manifestation.

Joseph's response to his brothers when they came to Egypt was a clear demonstration that the process God took him through was effective. It had made him humble, sober, and disciplined. Most people would seek revenge against the people who treat them badly, especially when they have the power to do so. Instead, Joseph forgave them. It takes a great amount of self-restraint for a man of power and authority to not pay back the people who threw him in a pit and later sold him into slavery.

The process produced fulfillment of the dreams he had as a teenager. God knew what was going to happen when He gave Joseph the two dreams. Although, at the time there was nothing to indicate that the content of the dreams was going to happen. He was the youngest among his brothers and had not traveled anywhere apart from his family. There was nothing to suggest that he was going to be great; yet, God knew everything, and God knew He would sustain Joseph through the process.

No matter what you are going through, when the opportunity presents, go out of your way to help someone, because you do not know who that person will be tomorrow.

> **When it is your time, when your season arrives, no number of liars can stand in the way. Even people who have information against you cannot lift a tongue against you, because God will condemn them. That is the evidence that your divine season has come.**

CHANGE YOUR GARMENT

When your season comes, change will be quick and overnight. Joseph shaved and changed clothes. The problem for many is that when their season comes, they do not want to change. They remain in prison because they are stubborn and do not want to change. You cannot go into the new season with the same attitude, concepts, and perceptions. You need to know the code of dressing for the events of life. Joseph shaved, removed his prison garment, and dressed for where he was going, not where he was leaving.

Joseph's story leaves us with an uncontestable truth: God is sovereign and no man can stop what He is doing in your life. God orchestrated human history such that, by natural acts, it initially did not suggest anything extraordinary. Joseph's brothers had to travel to Egypt to buy food because of the famine that came upon the earth. That famine was part of God setting the stage for Joseph's brothers to come and bow before him, and later his mother and father, and the entire tribe of Jacob. That is the God of process I am talking about!

Joseph's story affirms that whatever God decides to do with you, if only you are willing to go through the process, it will manifest irrespective of any negative human blockades and interruptions.

Beloved always keep in mind when you are passing through the fire, the waters, and the rivers, that God is with you, and when your process is over, your end shall be better than your beginning (Isa 43:2).

When you are down, when it looks like you have fallen in the battle of destiny, when adversity rides over your head like horsemen, don't give in to despair. Set your mind on the image God has given you concerning your future. Learn to see the presence and not the absence of God. Keep faith and do not defer your hope (Pro 13:12), but cultivate a strong desire and be determined to hold on until the process finishes its work in you.

Chapter 4: Process Builds Capacity

There is always a time gap between intentions and the actualization of what is intended. The story of David's life provides a credible example from which we can learn.

Time to be Anointed

If you follow the story well, you will realize that Samuel anointed David at a young age. David had been busy taking care of his father's sheep in the wilderness. No one at that time would imagine him as the king of Israel. Even when Samuel went to Jesse's house to anoint him as the man after God's heart, David was not home. Jesse told Samuel those were all of his male children.

Upon Samuel's insistence, Jesse remembered David was in the wilderness. As soon as David appeared, God told Samuel that David was His choice. **In that humble home, the prophet of God anointed one who became the greatest king that Israel ever had** (1 Sam 16:13).

We know that David did not immediately move into the palace to become king (2 Sam 5:4). A process must kick in by all means. He had to wait for the fullness of the time to come, like Jesus had to wait for the fullness of the time. God had to set the stage, but David had to also build capacity for ruling a nation as God's cherished king.

Not much was said again about the anointed David until the giant, Goliath, started hurling insults against God. When all the men of Israel were afraid to answer Goliath, this boy dared the giant (1 Sam 17:41-44).

Saul offered David his battle armor, but David could not use them because he had not built the capacity to use metal armors. What he knew then was the armor that comes from the anointing of the Holy Spirit. It's the anointing by which a man uses his hands to kill a lion and a bear to save his flock.

You know the story. David won his first open feat and it was tremendous! He killed the uncircumcised Philistine and removed the shame of Israel. For many, that was the opportune time to campaign for the position of leader of the nation. He easily would have won if he did that. Remember the women had already started singing "Saul hath slain his thousands, and David his ten thousand" (1 Sam 18:7). They were accurate by the facts of the situation, but the truth is that God was not yet done with David. He had not exercised himself in the ways of a king yet.

He built some capacity taking care of flock in the desert, but had not yet learned how to translate that into taking care of God's people. That was just another phase of the process.

TIME TO LEARN TO BE KING

By God's design, David was brought to the palace where he would be king. That was an opportunity to also see what was involved in leading a nation. He must have a taste of how decisions are made and executed. It was still not time to be king because the process was not yet completed.

David had to learn to use his musical gift and anointing to soothe the woes of a king who had lived in disobedience. Now, the king's welfare was in the hands of the prospective king. David could have pushed for the throne that was already his but he knew he had more to learn.

Saul became envious of David. The Scripture says

> "And Saul sought to smite David even to the wall with the javelin; but he slipped away out of Saul's presence, and he smote the javelin into the wall: and David fled, and escaped that night." (1 Sam 19:10)

He had to learn also to be humble and endure the anger of a king who was then afraid and suspicious of him. The escape of the javelin and the events that followed underscore the role of his process.

> **Like David, God is able to deliver you from any adverse situation that is calculated to terminate your assignment.**

This led David to write in Psalm 18:17, "He delivered me from my strong enemy, and from them which hated me: for they were too strong for me."

LEARNING TO LOVE AND HONOR GOD

David became a vagabond running away from the palace where he would be king and from the king who sought to end his life. At a point David had all the opportunity to kill Saul, and if he had, in today's legal system, he would be pardoned for self-defense. For David, it was not time for self-defense. It was an opportunity to learn to honor God's anointed. He recognized that it was God who anointed Saul, and would not be responsible for his death.

> **You have to respect God's anointed because one day you may be in the same position and expect people to respect the anointing upon your life. That is an unchanging principle.**

David aligned himself with Israel's enemies. That became an opportunity to develop loyalty. David was spared going to war against his own people, had not the Philistines intervened (1 Sam 29).

Throughout all these events, God's time had not yet come. David was going through experiences that corporately could best be described as training ground.

David had to learn until the process was finished, to finally be installed as King of Israel. When he became king, it still was not yet over. He had to learn some lessons the hard way. Learning the hard way is also part of the process.

In Psalm 51, David wrote his prayer of confession for adultery and murder. The lesson he learned via God's prophet, Nathan, was that as a king you don't compete with your subjects over property. That is not the way of a king. David was still learning.

Throughout the process David was exposed to numerous encounters with God. In the Psalms, we get a clear picture of what those encounters produced in David. It is no wonder that no one writes about worship like him. David was the greatest worshipper of all time.

Many of today's praise and worship leaders are mostly singers and rarely encounter God like the Psalmist did. They use their skills, but David worshipped from his experiences. That makes a significant difference and can be easily attributed to going through the process.

> A process is training ground meant to strengthen your muscles, sharpen your vision, build capacity in you, and give you opportunity to properly psyche yourself for the task ahead of you.

THE NAVY SEALS EXPERIENCE

The differences between the Navy Seals and other soldiers are training and processes. Not every soldier can, or desires to, endure the process that Navy Seals go through. This includes but is not limited to swimming four to five times a week, running that risks injuries to their legs, weight lifting, moving their own body weight, sit-ups and push-ups and pull-ups, stretching exercises, etc. You have to go through these if you hope to serve as a Navy Seal.

"Guys come here to better themselves through adversity, they come here to win. Nobody pays for a course to lose or feel bad about themselves, nobody comes here to take last place, get embarrassed, or be humiliated".[2]

What do they gain? They develop a powerful new outlook, a fresh mind-set, and readiness to conquer life's toughest challenges. They learn that no matter the obstacle in front of them, nor the wall they face, to persevere: they go over, under, and around. They fight, and fight hard for everything. Trainees are made to understand that nothing can stop them, except themselves!

In one of the courses, a seven-day training takes participants through what is called "Hell night". The

---

[2] *Extreme Seal Experience. Retrieved July 2019 from http://www.extremesealexperience.com/*

objective of Hell Night is to build confidence and teamwork. It is believed that there is something inside each of us, something very deep, a side that we never knew existed. That demanding, grueling, 24-hour ordeal is intended to bring it out.

David's process, his endurance of unpleasant and challenging circumstances, can be likened to a Navy Seals training session. He survived rough, dangerous, and potentially devastating conditions, to build the capacity needed to lead God's people.

Chapter 5: Process Refines You

From Fishermen to Fishers of Men

We are privileged to know the truth of God by which all men can be saved, thanks to the steadfastness of the early apostles of Jesus Christ. They were stoned, tormented, sawn asunder, slain with sword, mocked, and thrown into lion dens; yet, none of those things could make them give up the faith they developed in Jesus Christ.

We owe them a lot. The writer of Hebrews says that we are not worthy of them. Take time to read this to get the picture.

> "And what shall I more say? for the time would fail me to tell of Gideon, and of Barak, and of Samson, and of Jephtha; of David also, and Samuel, and of the prophets: Who through faith subdued kingdoms, wrought righteousness, obtained promises, stopped the mouths of lions. Quenched the violence of fire, escaped the edge of the sword, out of weakness were made strong, waxed valiant in fight, turned to flight the armies of the

aliens. Women received their dead raised to life again: and others were tortured, not accepting deliverance; that they might obtain a better resurrection: And others had trial of cruel mockings and scourgings, yea, moreover of bonds and imprisonment: They were stoned, they were sawn asunder, were tempted, were slain with the sword: they wandered about in sheepskins and goatskins; being destitute, afflicted, tormented; (Of whom the world was not worthy:) they wandered in deserts, and in mountains, and in dens and caves of the earth. And these all, having obtained a good report through faith, received not the promise: God having provided some better thing for us, that they without us should not be made perfect." (Heb 11:32-40)

A few years earlier, these could not be said of them. Now, let us examine what the disciples of Jesus went through.

UNLEARNED, RAW, FISHERMEN

These were mostly unlearned men. Only a few had some formal education. The leader of the group was a fisherman who very often spoke before he thought about what he would say. They were not Pharisees or Sadducees who had studied the law from cover to cover. No one acknowledged them. In fact, some of them were considered serious sinners by their society. These were the men whom Jesus chose to leave the destiny of the world.

The fact that we have Christianity today, indicates that the disciples did not fail. They delivered as Jesus envisaged. The reason is simple. These men went through the process. They spent three and a half years with Jesus. They went with Him everywhere. They saw Him teach, preach, heal, and deliver people from the domination of demons. They saw Him handle different human situations with different approaches. They received rebukes from their Master for lack of faith and lack of understanding of spiritual truth. In all these, they humbled themselves and went through the discipleship process.

Is that what gave Jesus the confidence to leave the destiny of the world in their hands? It was not their academic prowess, nor their social standing, nor their financial wealth of prosperity -- many of them had few possessions. They even left their means of livelihood to follow a much younger man.

> **Going through the process has never been fun. The disciples submitted themselves to a process that would make them the leaders of the world. Their creed would become one that no humanistic philosophy can stand against. It is called The Gospel, and it has the power to deliver humanity from all of its woes.**

If you want to understand refinement, consider this example. During the period theologians call The Passion Week, all the disciples fled and went away in hiding for fear of their lives. Peter, who pledged going with Jesus all the way, betrayed Him and swore he did not know Jesus (Mark 14:66-72). We know he repented later. After the death of Jesus, their fear grew even more until the resurrection came.

The resurrection seemed to reignite fire in the disciples. Now they wanted to go and take their world. Jesus said they should wait because the process must be completed first. The Holy Spirit who would empower them was yet to be poured on them.

TRANSFORMED INTO WORLD CHANGERS

The Day of Pentecost came and we are witnesses to what followed. The fearful fisherman preached and 3,000 souls were saved in a day. The team went about preaching, teaching, healing, and their lives were also testifying that they were witnesses of Jesus Christ.

The once fearful men were asking the leaders to judge whether they, or God, should be obeyed. Where was the fear? Where was the timidity? Where was the uncertainty? Gone, gone, gone! Those men walked with Jesus for three and a half years, and then experienced the outpouring of the Holy Spirit. All these did not happen over night. They had to go through process.

If you evaded the process you would be are raw, unrefined, prone to make mistakes, and likely to ruin whatever great thing God wants to do with your life. You would have no encounters with God, and no lessons learned. You might hear other people's testimonies and experiences in the Lord and memorize them, but they would not be yours.

> You may even preach about going through the process using all the testimonies of others you have heard. You might read about my testimony and use it to preach; yet, nothing compares to having your own encounters with God and learning of Him for yourself. Nothing substitutes that.

Jesus took His disciples through the complete process because they started as unlearned fishermen. Through the process He refined them, then He gave them power. Jesus knew what harm could come to someone unrefined if you gave him power. He had to break them to humble them.

I don't think it is a wise decision to go around this process. You must patiently go through for yourself.

Process Yields Value

The process determines the value of a product. Gold is not gold until it has been refined in fire. You will sometimes find yourself in a dark place. However, do not despair because you are going through the fire so God can refine you to be effective for the Kingdom (Psa 119:71). God's process requires you to go through the fire so you can be conformed into the image of Christ. You may be in the middle of a process right now that looks like the lowest valley possible, but God will never leave you in the process and when you get through it, you will be victorious.

When I see people with heights and no spiritual depth to maintain the height, I remember that height does not maintain heights. I am concerned when someone is at a height without depth because it is a position that they will not be able to maintain. Go through the process so you can yield value and be fruitful to the Kingdom. It will require process to gain the depth to sustain the height and bear fruit for the kingdom.

Chapter 6: Process Guarantees God Encounters

Knowing God in the Process

"And such as do wickedly against the covenant shall he corrupt by flatteries: but the people that do know their God shall be strong, and do exploits." (Dan 11:32)

You can listen to a man talk and conclude to what extent he may have had encounters with God. Encountering God differentiates those who know God from those who don't know God. Throughout the Bible, there are several examples of what encountering God did to people. I have decided to discuss a few of them in this chapter to see what lessons we can learn from their experiences.

Moses Encounters the God of Power

Can you believe that for 40 years after fleeing Egypt out of fear of being killed, Moses had to enroll in God's school? He did not understand that 40 years of keeping the flock of Jethro was training for 40 years of taking care of God's people.

God must have taught him a lot even before the dramatic encounter on Mount Sinai. The encounter was clear. It was without any doubts and there he received his mandate, his mission, and the message God wanted His children to hear. If you are not sure of your mandate, your mission, and message, you are not ready to lead God's people.

Moses saw the ten plagues that came upon Egypt, with none of them happening to the Israelites. He saw the mighty deliverance of the first born that established the Passover. He saw God's hand divide the Red Sea for Israel when the same sea drowned the Egyptians when they dared to cross. He saw Israel defeat the Amalekites for as long as his hands were up on the day of battle.

> **Moses saw a raw demonstration of God's power throughout the 40 years he led God's people. His encounter was possible because he submitted to the process**

Perhaps you now understand why he argued with God that if God's presence would not go with them, then God should not send them beyond.

"And he said, My presence shall go with thee, and I will give thee rest. And he said unto him,

If thy presence go not with me, carry us not up hence. For wherein shall it be known here that I and thy people have found grace in thy sight? is it not in that thou goest with us? so shall we be separated, I and thy people, from all the people that are upon the face of the earth." (Exo 33:14-16)

What you have to understand is that it is only a man who has had encounters with God who can make such declarations or pleas with God. If you have not seen God's hand, you cannot talk that way. It is all a process.

> **In the first 40 years of his life, Moses learned the ways of the world in Egypt. In the next 40 years of his life, he learned the ways of a shepherd, taking care of flock. Thus, he was not even aware that 80 years of his life was preparation. The next 40 years of his life was yet another phase where he had to go through the process to know Yahweh as the only true, powerful God.**

This was a man described as the meekest on earth. Process made him meek. He had to go through God's process. He came to know God's power, probably like no other man.

DAVID ENCOUNTERS THE GOD WORTHY OF ALL WORSHIP

How do we know if David encountered God? To answer this question for yourself, I urge you to chronologically read the books of Samuel and Chronicles that capture the life of David. In addition, read the book of Psalms. The Psalms are full of declarations of the characteristics of God.

The Psalmist and king wrote countless descriptions of God in his songs. The question is, *How did he get all that information?* We know that the Holy Spirit inspired the Scriptures so we can read them and know about God. David, in addition, wrote a lot about his experiences with God.

> **There is always a difference between hearing about God, reading about God in the Scriptures, and encountering God. That is an experience no man can take from you, and it is the portion for those who want to go through the process.**

David fought with a lion and a bear to save his sheep when they were attacked. That was an experience of the power of God at work. How many of you have fought even with an attacking dog?

David saw the power of God again when he killed Goliath. Many people have their version of what happened. Some say David was very skillful so he could target the small space in the helmet of Goliath. Others have other descriptions. Consider what David said to King Saul prior to killing Goliath:

> "David said moreover, The LORD that delivered me out of the paw of the lion, and out of the paw of the bear, he will deliver me out of the hand of this Philistine. And Saul said unto David, Go, and the LORD be with thee." (1 Sam 17:37)

Ponder what he told Goliath before killing him:

> "Then said David to the Philistine, Thou comest to me with a sword, and with a spear, and with a shield: but I come to thee in the name of the Lord of hosts, the God of the armies of Israel, whom thou hast defied. This day will the Lord deliver thee into mine hand; and I will smite thee, and take thine head from thee; and I will give the carcasses of the host of the Philistines this day unto the fowls

of the air, and to the wild beasts of the earth; that all the earth may know that there is a God in Israel. And all this assembly shall know that the Lord saveth not with sword and spear: for the battle is the Lord's, and he will give you into our hands." (1 Sam 17:45-47)

Let this put to silence any discussion on how David killed the giant! The truth is clear. Glory be to God.

David in the palace saw the divine deliverance of God on those occasions when King Saul threw spears at him, intending to make an end of the life of God's anointed. Remember when David had opportunity to kill Saul? He did not because he had learned of God and His ways, and knew that you don't touch God's anointed. People in our generation who have not encountered God say and do all manner of things against God's anointed. David's encounters with God taught Him the hand and favor upon God's anointed.

The process that led to his installation as King of Israel was challenging. Throughout it, he saw God's protection and provision, including times he had to disguise himself as a mad man, his experiences with

Abigail and Nabal, and his enemies' attempts to get him to fight against Israel.

Did you hear what he told his wife, Michal, when she rebuked him for dancing to celebrate the return of the ark of God to Israel?

> *"Then David returned to bless his household. And Michal the daughter of Saul came out to meet David, and said, How glorious was the king of Israel to day, who uncovered himself to day in the eyes of the handmaids of his servants, as one of the vain fellows shamelessly uncovereth himself! And David said unto Michal, It was before the LORD, which chose me before thy father, and before all his house, to appoint me ruler over the people of the LORD, over Israel: therefore will I play before the LORD. And I will yet be more vile than thus, and will be base in mine own sight: and of the maidservants which thou hast spoken of, of them shall I be had in honour. Therefore Michal the daughter of Saul had no child unto the day of her death."*
> (2 Sam 6:20-23)

David saw God's hand in his life as a king in several ways. Many of these are captured in his Psalms, which are actually his praise and worship repertoire. What is your repertoire of praise and worship coming out of encounters with God?

> **How ready are you to go through the process to discover God? Simply praying, "Open the eyes of my heart, Lord I want to see You" is not enough. It is not a guarantee that you will know God. It is not a visual picture of God you want to see. You want to know Him through experience.**

Having an instant vision like Isaiah had when King Uzziah died (Isa 6:1-8) is okay, but you need a lifestyle encounter with God via all the circumstances of your life. That makes the difference.

DANIEL ENCOUNTERS THE GOD OF WISDOM AND SUPREMACY

Read the story of Daniel again. Here was a Jewish boy taken into captivity because his fathers disobeyed God's commands and broke His covenant with them. Recap his experiences. Daniel passed the first test in refusing to compromise what he knew to be healthy eating according to Jewish standards, taught in the Law of Moses.

Daniel prayed to his God, and he was reported to the king who had decreed that no man should pray to another God other than the gods of the land of Babylon. The king decided that Daniel should go into the lion's den as punishment. He did not know that the Lion of the tribe of Judah is a superior lion.

As if that was not enough, the king decided to make a golden image and he commanded everyone to bow and worship that image at certain times. Three Hebrew boys who had witnessed Daniel's deliverance from the lion's den decided they would not bow, even at the threat of death. That was another encounter of God for Daniel.

Daniel interpreted the king's dream with wisdom. The king's wise men and magicians were clueless.

Then Nebuchadnezzar died and his son reigned in his stead. This young king had the audacity of using the vessels of the temple in a party he organized for his lords. We know the experience of the hand that wrote on the wall. It took a Daniel full of wisdom and understanding in dreams to interpret. That same night, Daniel's interpretation happened live!

Does it come as a surprise that Daniel should write, they "that do know their God shall be strong, and do exploits" (Dan 11:32)?

Daniel had learned all his life to be a Jew and to keep his faith in God regardless of circumstances. He was in the palace so he was better off than his other brethren; yet, he vowed not to defile himself. Holiness unto the Lord is a process and Daniel knew that too well. Now you can understand why God also promoted him and made him see His power and walked in His wisdom. How are you positioning yourself in the process to know God for yourself?

PETER ENCOUNTERS THE GOD OF IMMACULATE NATURE

From fisherman to fishers of men, Peter encountered God (Luke 5:1-11). Let's examine his process: promising to go with Jesus all the way, a statement he probably made out of his flesh; repentance; forgiveness received from Jesus; encountering the resurrection; witnessing Jesus enter their room when all doors were locked; all the miracles he saw Jesus perform; the transfiguration; and the hasty statement to build three tabernacles for Jesus, Moses, and Elijah. All were his encounters with God in the process of becoming the leader of the early church.

Peter, on a number of occasions, saw himself in the light of Jesus and acknowledged himself as a man of unclean lips. He saw Jesus as the Christ, the Son of the Living God. He saw Jesus at the Transfiguration in His full glory. He also was part of the team that asked, "What manner of man is this that the winds and the waves obey Him" (Matt 8:27). These were experiences of his encounter and no man could take them away from him.

Now you can understand why he requested to be crucified upside down as the historians would have us learn.

> **It is not enough for us to read these and the next day start running all over the place, expecting God to follow us like our armor bearers follow us today. The point of revelation of a truth about God is only the beginning.**

When your eyes are opened by the Holy Spirit to know and understand God's truth, it is often just the beginning. It just means it's time to go through the process to experience what you just read about God.

When you run ahead of God, your experience may be like the sons of Sceva; and the devils will ask you, "we know of Jesus and Paul and so-and-so, but who are you (Acts 19:15)? You need your own encounters with God. Only those who go through God's process are guaranteed to be made great.

PAUL ENCOUNTERS THE GOD OF GREAT SALVATION

When Saul of Tarsus was persecuting the church, he had no clue that he was a chosen vessel. God's ways are always higher than ours (Isa 55:9). I am sure the church then was praying that something terrible would happen to Saul so their troubles would come to an end. For God, it was a process. The process was that Saul should develop hatred for the church so much that when his eyes were opened, he would transfer the same zeal into loving God's people and doing God's work.

His experience on the way to Damascus and the events that followed, including time he spent searching the Scriptures, all contributed to the success of his ministry and service as one of the greatest Christians ever.

Remember that Paul wrote a lot about patient endurance. He always had to wait for God to deliver.

Out of his encounters with God, Paul came to know Him as the one who would have all men come to the knowledge of the truth and be saved. He knew the God of Salvation and of grace, and he unapologetically articulated his faith and commitment to Jesus Christ. Paul saw himself as the chief of sinners. Hence, the grace of God meant so much to him.

Everywhere he went the message of God's love and salvation to mankind did not depart from his lips. Paul taught more about the grace of God than any Christian.

CHAPTER 7: PROCESS PRODUCES FAITH AND STABILITY

One of the challenges of the church today is the misunderstanding of faith. Many are of the following mindset: God has said it; I have faith it is going to happen as He said; therefore, I can start making it happen. A common example is the way many modern day pastors use the phrase, "by this time tomorrow". It has become a regular phrase for many who consider themselves a person of faith and a great prophet. I think if they learn the history and processes that led to God working that great miracle, a greater understanding would come.

> For many, faith substitutes for going through the process of God. That is a great error. Faith is required for the initiation of the process, and going through the process in turn builds and perfects one's faith. Going through process is not against faith. It helps faith and perfects it.

FAITH DOES NOT REPLACE THE PROCESS

The Bible clearly indicates there are levels of faith, or measures of faith. These levels are definitely the result of process. Our level of faith is directly proportional to our encounters with God, which is also directly related to the extent to which they are committed to God's processes of this life.

I can say with certainty that faith is developed out of the process. If you have not gone through the process that refines your faith, to remove all the fantasy and presumptuousness that sometimes goes in the name of faith, you could even make a shipwreck of your faith.

JOB'S FAITH THROUGH PROCESS

The story of Job stands as one that establishes the relationship between faith and process. This man already believed in God. That is why he offered sacrifices for his children on a regular basis, in case they had committed any sins against God.

God decided to let Satan take him through a process. You are familiar with the story. It was a difficult experience for Job. The story does not say the exact duration, but anyone who is familiar with a process knows one thing about a process – it takes time.

For all the time Job went through the process he was armed with one thing: that when God had tried him, he would come out as pure gold. That statement is about both an increase in his faith in God, and his character as a child of God. Why are we reading about Job today? He went through a process that confirmed his faith in God.

> **Process is not antagonistic to faith. So, have faith in God, but let that faith go through the process for it to be strengthened, and gain stability as a Christian.**

When you hear the word of God and you go through the process, your faith is purified, challenged and strengthened. That is how measures of faith come about.

Sometimes people around you may become tired of watching your process and will encourage you to be discouraged. Their words and attitude are designed to make you weary in your mind, to give up, because you are seen as a burden to them. That was the case with Job's wife.

Not everyone will understand your process. Eliphaz, Bildad, Zophar, and even Job's wife, had no insight or foresight about why Job was going through his process.

Job's wife must have been getting tired of caring for him during his affliction, worn out by the weight of it all. Job's wife encouraged him to cut the process short by simply provoking God, in the hope that God in His anger would strike him dead, thus, bringing relief both to her husband and herself. Whatever the motivation, she lacked the ability to see the outcome of the process.

From Job's wife's utterances, we can see that the process you go through can affect those around you, your loved ones, family, and friends. They can either become invaluable agents of support or instruments of terminating the process.

> Be mindful of who counsels you and who influences you during your season of process.

GOD HAS SET THE LIMITS TO YOUR PROCESS

"And the LORD said unto Satan, Behold, all that he hath is in thy power; only upon himself put not forth thine hand." (Job 1:12)

"And brake up for it my decreed place, and set bars and doors, And said, Hitherto shalt thou come, but no further: and here shall thy proud waves be stayed?" (Job 38:10 -11)

"There hath no temptation taken you but such as is common to man: but God is faithful, who will not suffer you to be tempted above that ye are able; but will with the temptation also make a way to escape, that ye may be able to bear it." (1 Cor 10:13)

Temptations and falling into sin are all diabolic strategies of the enemy to gain advantage over you. They are calculated to make you lose your confidence in the providence of God and, thereby, give up on the process.

Don't lose your sanctification. Keep yourself pure. When you fall, repent, rise again and go through God's restoration process.

God will never let you be pushed past your limit. For every "thorn in the flesh", there is the sufficiency of His Grace (2 Cor 12:7-9).

When Job was tried and tested, he did not fight the process. The Word says, "In all this Job sinned not, nor charged God foolishly" (Job 1:22).

> **The Potter is still in charge and is the master of your process. God is still in control of your circumstances. He has predetermined how far your process must go.**

Don't fight the process. Even if it was orchestrated by the enemy and intended for evil, God can turn it around for your good.

> **May the keys to the bars and doors of your process be taken out of the hands of the enemy. By Divine authority, I arrest every ungodly wave assigned against you beyond the limits of your predetermined process!**

WITHSTANDING THE WINDS AND THE FLOODS

Jesus told a story in Matthew (7:24-27) of two men building their house. The first man built his house on sand. This man was called foolish, because sand does not have what it takes to hold a building, though it is easy to dig. You do not go through any process to build on sand. Let's look at what happened because he refused to go through the process.

> *"And the rain descended, and the floods came, and the winds blew, and beat upon*

that house; and it fell: and great was the fall of it." (Matt 7:27)

The house was leveled to the ground by the storm and the winds.

Now, look at the second man who built his house on a rock. He was called wise because he built his house on a solid foundation. There is a laborious process that you have to go through to build on a rock. It takes diligence, time, and endurance. Rock is hard, and it takes a process to break the rock and build a foundation on it so the building can stand. Jesus, in Matthew (7:25), completed the story:

> *"And the rain descended, and the floods came, and the winds blew, and beat upon that house; and it fell not: for it was founded upon a rock."*

The wind could not blow the house down like it did the house built on sand. Wind stands for change. When you go through the process you will be able to withstand the wind when it comes. Faith is further strengthened by the storms. You, too, are guaranteed God's blessings; however, if you try to take a shortcut you will be overtaken by the wind because you did not go through the process to build a strong foundation of faith.

Anyone who intends to build a high building understands that you need a deep foundation. The deeper your foundation the higher your building can go and the longer it will stand. A deep foundation guarantees longevity of your building.

> **Faith in God's word does not only guarantee stability but it also guarantees longevity, which then draws from going through processes God has established.**

Let your faith in God produce trust in God's ability to keep and preserve you, enable you to go through the challenges of life, overcome all the difficulties that come your way, and still remain standing.

God commanded us to "Put on the whole armour of God, that ye may be able to stand against the wiles of the devil" (Eph 6:11). And having done all, stand. Make sure you are standing on the Rock.

> *"And the remnant that is escaped of the house of Judah shall again take root downward, and bear fruit upward"* (Isa 37:31).

Process purifies your faith, makes it strong, and enables you to fight the warfare of faith, "Casting down imaginations, and every high thing that exalteth itself against the knowledge of God, and bringing into captivity every thought to the obedience of Christ" (2 Cor 10:5).

Imaginations are "reasonings". You will have to learn the art of casting down every thought and imagination that exalts itself above the mind of God for your life. Do not be deterred by the reasoning of men. Put your faith and trust in the Author and Finisher of your faith. Do not be weary in your mind. For the scripture says, "Whosoever believeth on him shall not be ashamed" (Rom 10:11).

Take a bold step of faith and contend for your destiny. Overthrow every imposition, fear, contention, controversy, and confusion. Wrestle in prayer and overcome every impediment that is designed to force you to bypass your process.

CHAPTER 8: PROCESS – CLAY IN THE POTTER'S HAND

So far, I have tried to help you understand the value of going through the process. Now, I want to focus on realities about going through the process. It is easy for the believer to attribute every unpleasant thing that comes his way to the devil. Their philosophy is that if you are a believer in Christ, you should not experience any difficulty. This is far from the truth. God's processes for refining you are a mix of all kinds of situations and circumstances, some you will not enjoy.

The writer of Hebrews says:

"And ye have forgotten the exhortation which speaketh unto you as unto children, My son, despise not thou the chastening of the Lord, nor faint when thou art rebuked of him: For whom the Lord loveth he chasteneth, and scourgeth every son whom he receiveth. If ye endure chastening, God dealeth with you as with sons; for what son is he whom the father chasteneth not? But if ye be without chastisement, whereof all are partakers, then are ye bastards, and not sons. Furthermore

we have had fathers of our flesh which corrected us, and we gave them reverence: shall we not much rather be in subjection unto the Father of spirits, and live? For they verily for a few days chastened us after their own pleasure; but he for our profit, that we might be partakers of his holiness. Now no chastening for the present seemeth to be joyous, but grievous: nevertheless afterward it yieldeth the peaceable fruit of righteousness unto them which are exercised thereby." (Heb 12:5-11)

JEREMIAH AT THE POTTER

I am sure you are familiar with Jeremiah's experience at the potters.

"The word which came to Jeremiah from the LORD, saying, Arise, and go down to the potter's house, and there I will cause thee to hear my words. Then I went down to the potter's house, and, behold, he wrought a work on the wheels. And the vessel that he made of clay was marred in the hand of the

potter: so he made it again another vessel, as seemed good to the potter to make it. Then the word of the LORD came to me, saying, O house of Israel, cannot I do with you as this potter? saith the LORD. Behold, as the clay is in the potter's hand, so are ye in mine hand, O house of Israel" (Jer 18:1-6).

YOU ARE CLAY IN THE POTTER'S HAND

"But now, O LORD, thou art our father; we are the clay, and thou our potter; and we all are the work of thy hand" (Isa 64:8).

The first reality of process that you must know, understand, and accept, is that you are like clay in the potter's hand. God is the potter and you are the clay. He determines what He wants to make of you, not the other way. There is a process that the clay goes through to eventually become pottery that people can purchase for different uses. God takes you through a similar process to make you what He wants you to be.

Let me take you through what the clay goes through in the potter's hands so you can relate with what God takes you through to perfect you for greatness.

Step 1: Selecting the Clay

The potter starts the process by selecting the clay. In John (15:16), Jesus said, "Ye have not chosen me, but I have chosen you, and ordained you, that ye should go and bring forth fruit, and that your fruit should remain".

> **You need to understand that you did not choose yourself. God chose you and predetermined what He wanted to do with you. You do not give God instructions as some may think.**

Child of God, you have been divinely selected by God, a vessel "meet" for His purpose.

> *"But in a great house there are not only vessels of gold and of silver, but also of wood and of earth; and some to honour, and some to dishonour. If a man therefore purge himself from these, he shall be a vessel unto honour, sanctified, and meet for the master's*

use, and prepared unto every good work."
(2 Tim 2:20-21)

How you are processed will determine what kind of vessel you become. Will you be a vessel of Gold or Earth, honour or dishonor? Note that the process each of these vessels will have to go through will depend on its intended use.

When clay is selected, the potter moves to the next stage in which he takes the unnecessary particles out of the clay, which may include grass, dirt, sand, etc.

The particles represent our old nature. The old nature must be thoroughly dealt with for anyone to look like Christ. Dealing with the old nature is not instant. It is a process. God takes anyone who comes to Christ through a process that ends in being conformed to the image of Christ (Rom 8:29). The Holy Spirit is the executor of that process. By His power, the believer is transformed into Christ's image.

Can you imagine the clay talking back at the potter or telling the potter what he should take out and what he should leave? It does not happen like that. The potter has absolute control over everything that happens to the clay at the point of purification.

> **Check your attitude as you abide in God's molding fingers. That will determine how long you stay in the process.**

Step 2: Mixing the Clay

The mixing of the clay with water is the second step. The water helps soften the clay and help you form the clay for its purpose. The water represents the Word of God in our lives. The Word of God is necessary to break down every stony heart and build Christ like character to prepare us for the purpose that was predestined in our lives (Jer 1:5).

The mixing of water to clay helps making the clay soft and malleable. As water is added, the potter keeps pounding until the clay is soft enough. This is the part of the process where we think God has forsaken us by virtue of the pounding. You may be wondering why God has left you, but the truth is that He is there. Listen to what He said through the Prophet Isaiah"

> "When thou passest through the waters, I
> will be with thee; and through the rivers, they

shall not overflow thee: when thou walkest through the fire, thou shalt not be burned; neither shall the flame kindle upon thee." (Isa 43:2)

God planned for you to go through fire because there is no other way by which you can become the great person you want to be. That is why He gives you the assurance of His presence in the fire and through the waters. You will not die. Many great people have gone through. You are not the only one.

Step 3: Forming the Clay

The next part of the process is where the potter creates the shape of the object to be made. The potter can use a spinning wheel, coiling method, or by hand to create the shape. God uses all methods during the process to conform us to Christ.

The spinning wheel represents the seasons we go through as part of our process. You have to understand that spinning is not fun. Try turning yourself in a very fast way. You may feel dizzy and think you are going to fall and hurt yourself. That is what the potter does. The potter's wheel is a spinning device. It turns you round and round and round, for as long as the process requires.

The beautiful thing about spinning is that God shapes you as He spins you on His wheel. You must willingly surrender in His hands to be conformed and survive the process. There are times when God will slow down the process and times when He will take you faster.

At the beginning of our Christian life, the Holy Spirit will gently nudge us to the right way and during these times we should desire God's word to get through that process (1 Pet 2:2). As we grow spiritually, we may have to go through different types of processes to mature to the next level.

Step 4: Cutting and Shaping the Clay

When the clay is formed, the potter then cuts the clay to finalize the shape and refine the edges. God takes us through the same process as He shapes us from the inside and out. This process is where God spiritually circumcises us, cutting away those things that do not bring glory to His name. They are the pleasures of this world, idols that we worship, or unhealthy behaviors that we are reluctant to release.

You have to yield to the process by allowing yourself to be shaped into Christ's character because the evil one always tries to get you fight against the process. Paul captured this in his personal experience when he wrote:

> "For I do not do the good I want, but the evil I do not want is what I keep on doing. Now if I do what I do not want, it is no longer I who do it, but sin that dwells within me. So, I find it to be a law that when I want to do right, evil lies close at hand." (Rom 7:19-21)

Step 5: Raising the Temperature

During this stage, the potter places the formed clay in the kiln for 12 or more hours and then it is removed for cooling. This kiln will bake until the clay becomes hard. When potter sees a crack, he does not patch it. He will start all over again.

Gold (Au) melts at a temperature of 1,064° C, while silver (Ag), melts when heated to 962 °C. It requires a higher temperature to melt gold than silver.

Understandably, silver is lighter and less noble in comparison to gold

The intensity of your process may be a clue to the vessel God is making out of you. Do not fight the process but rather, "endure hardness as a good solider of Jesus Christ" (2 Tim 2:3). The Lord says through His prophet in Isaiah (48:10), "Behold, I have refined thee, but not with silver; I have chosen thee in the furnace of affliction". The fire will test your character and patience as God is prepares you to prevail in the stormy days. You have to die daily in the fire (I Cor 15:31). Going through the kiln of life is a discipline that God will repeat until He gets you right. God does not patch you if He sees cracks in your life. He renews you over and over until He perfects your look.

Then the clay goes on the shelf to cool down. This is the process when you experience some success and accomplishments as you are fully living for Christ, and you can say with the Apostle Paul, "I am crucified with Christ: nevertheless I live; yet not I, but Christ liveth in me: and the life which I now live in the flesh I live by the faith of the Son of God, who loved me, and gave himself for me" (Gal 2:20).

At this point you have matured in Christ and you notice that you are speaking more maturely, treating people more like a Christian, and you no longer engage in some kinds of communications, because you have become both light and salt.

> **What began as clay, looking like dirt, is now a beautiful display in the King's palace where everyone admires your accomplished greatness.**

Do you want this type of admiration and greatness for your life? Then, do not fight the process. Remain malleable in the creative hands of God, the wisest Potter ever.

CHAPTER 9: PROCESS REALITIES

Let's now shift our attention to traits and requirements that enhance going through the process.

PROCESS REQUIRES CHRISTIAN CHARACTER

"But the fruit of the Spirit is love, joy, peace, longsuffering, gentleness, goodness, faith, Meekness, temperance: against such there is no law." (Gal 5:22-23)

The Bible describes God's Word as a two-edged sword (Heb 4:12). Many principles of faith in God's word are like that. For example, process produces Christian character, but character is also needed to go through the process. The primary factor that makes people give up and not complete the process is lack of Christian character. Let's take a look at some of the character traits that are critical to going through the process.

Patience – Waiting until it Happens

Jacob leaves us with a graphic presentation of patience. He had labored seven years for Rachel, the wife of his heart. Laban deceived him, insisting he had to serve seven more years for Rachel. Jacob was ready to serve a total of 14 years to get the woman of his heart (Gen 29:20-28). That was a long wait.

Your guess could be as right as mine concerning what Jacob had to endure those extra seven years to marry Rachel. Still, that was not the end of the story. Jacob had to wait more years after that before Rachel could bear him a child. Of course, that child of Joseph's old age ended up being the Saviour of the tribe.

King David, who understands the principle of waiting for God to come through, also wrote:

> "I waited patiently for the LORD; he turned to me and heard my cry. He lifted me out of the slimy pit, out of the mud and mire; he set my feet on a rock and gave me a firm place to stand." (Psa 40:1-2)

The critical element in patience is the waiting. The prophet Isaiah also wrote "they that wait upon the Lord shall renew their strength" (Isa 40:31).

Longsuffering

Longsuffering is another word within the family of waiting. Think of longsuffering as the ability to endure adversity cheerfully with a slow tendency to react negatively to unpleasant circumstances. Longsuffering is the quality of forbearance and self-control, that shows itself, particularly, in a willingness to wait upon God and his will (Pro 19:11; Col 3:12; Pro 14:29, 16:32; Mat 6:14-15).

The greatest challenge is when we are not willing to wait. As parents, we often struggle in teaching our children to wait. In our attempts to spare them the suffering that accompanies waiting for the right time for their desires, we can turn them into weaklings who are unable to withstand even the slightest difficulty.

They grow into adults and some become pastors, and that attitude continues. They still cannot wait for God's timing, and as a result, cause havoc in the body of Christ. Please learn to wait.

Self-Control

The biblical definition of self-control is "ruling one's spirit". It involves using self-restraint, being slow to react, and keeping one's emotions, feelings, and behaviors within biblically acceptable confines. It also involves physical and emotional self-mastery, particularly, in situations of intense provocation or temptation (Gal 5:22-23; Tit 2:11-12; 1 Tim 3:2; Tit 2:2,5-6; 2 Pet 1:5-9).

The Apostle Paul taught about self-control in action. This is what he wrote:

> "Know ye not that they which run in a race run all, but one receiveth the prize? So run, that ye may obtain. And every man that striveth for the mastery is temperate in all things. Now they do it to obtain a corruptible crown; but we an incorruptible. I therefore so run, not as uncertainly; so fight I, not as one that beateth the air: But I keep under my body, and bring it into subjection: lest that by any means, when I have preached to others, I myself should be a castaway."
> (1 Cor 9:24-27).

Many well-meaning Christians have got themselves into trouble because they did not discipline their body. They allowed the flesh to slowly creep into their lifestyle until it was difficult to subdue their inordinate passions. The flesh must be crucified; else, it becomes empowered beyond control. Any Christian who controls his flesh is on the way to constant victory. This is what God wants us to know, speaking through the apostle Paul.

Humility

Humility depicts an attitude of lowliness and obedience. It involves recognizing that God makes me all I am and gives me all I have, through His abundant grace (Mic 6:8; Jam 4:10; 1 Pet 3:8; Exo 10:3; Pro 16:19).

The Apostle Paul presents the best picture of humility when he talked about Jesus. He penned:

> *"Let this mind be in you, which was also in Christ Jesus: Who, being in the form of God, thought it not robbery to be equal with God: But made himself of no reputation, and took upon him the form of a servant, and was made in the likeness of men: And being found in fashion as a man, he humbled himself, and became obedient unto death, even the death*

of the cross. Wherefore God also hath highly exalted him, and given him a name which is above every name: That at the name of Jesus every knee should bow, of things in heaven, and things in earth, and things under the earth; And that every tongue should confess that Jesus Christ is Lord, to the glory of God the Father." (Phil 2:5-11)

Deciding to take on human form is the greatest example in humility. When the same people for whom He was coming to die insulted Jesus, He simply moved on. There was no point. He did not retaliate. Jesus was led as a lamb to the slaughter, yet He did not open his mouth. He could have commanded angels to blindfold His accusers and persecutors; yet, He did not. This is a perfect example of both humility and meekness. This is the example He leaves for us all.

The instant that is often cited to show the humility of Jesus was when He washed the feet of His disciples (John 13:1–17). That is the epitome of true servant-leadership.

> **Jesus is the word that became flesh to live in the world He created. He subjected Himself to the elements of His creation and went through humiliation of the highest degree without vengeance. Now that is humility.**

Sometimes people are taken up with pride. That causes us to question what they have that is greater than Jesus, why they are unable to humble themselves, and why they don't go through God's process to refine them, build capacity in them, and prepare them fully for what He called them to be.

Peter exhorts us to be humble in the sight of God and He will exalt us in due time (1 Pet 5:6). The truth is that even when God exalts you, it is more of privilege for greater responsibility, than something to boast about.

If you remain humble before God, there is no limit to what He can do with you. Humbly go through the process and we will meet on the other side of a victorious Christian journey.

Process Demands Submission

Anything you become without the process, you did not earn. If it is not tested and tried, you eventually lose it. The first Adam didn't suffer the process, so he didn't value what he had. The second Adam did.

God first created Adam in His image and blessed him, then He gave Adam responsibility.

> "So God created man in his own image, in the image of God created he him; male and female created he them. And God blessed them, and God said unto them, Be fruitful, and multiply, and replenish the earth, and subdue it: and have dominion over the fish of the sea, and over the fowl of the air, and over every living thing that moveth upon the earth."
>
> (Gen 1:27-28)

Some Christians want to move ahead of God and before they are blessed they want to start taking dominion. They do not understand that they have to submit to the process.

A woman is created, but a wife is formed. Boys are created, but men are formed. The first Adam was created, not formed. The first Adam did not go through a process, which is one of the reasons why he failed. If we do not understand the difference between creation and formation, we will miss it. The scriptures say that He created us and formed us.

> *"But now thus saith the LORD that created thee, O Jacob, and he that formed thee, O Israel, Fear not: for I have redeemed thee, I have called thee by thy name; thou art mine. When thou passest through the waters, I will be with thee; and through the rivers, they shall not overflow thee: when thou walkest through the fire, thou shalt not be burned; neither shall the flame kindle upon thee."* (Isa 43:1-2)

The first 30 years of man's life are his learning years. That should constitute the years of being formed. You have to be properly formed before you start ministering to others. The second 30 years are his achieving years, and these show the extent to which he is formed. The next 30 years, which are his retiring years, gives opportunity to assemble what he has achieved. When he reaches the next 30, which are the departing years, he should be able to say as the apostle Paul, that he has fought the fight, kept the race and his crown of righteousness awaits him (2 Tim 4:7). If you are not properly formed in your early years, you may have nothing to talk about in the departing years.

Process Takes Time

I cannot overemphasize this principle. Think again about the time God promised the Messiah and the time He actually appeared on the earth to redeem man. They were thousands of years apart.

The microwave society we live in is not helping us, and when we succumb to instant things, we get out of the process because we feel it is taking too long.

I know the question in your head is: *"How long do I have to stay in the process?"* The answer is simple – for as long as God wants it to last. Better still, until God feels He has finished with you. You have to understand that God holds the times and the seasons and until He says it is done, it is not done.

God spoke to Jeremiah (25:9-11) about the 70 years of captivity of the Israelites. There were others who prophesied that it would be shorter. That is not how God works. If God knows it takes 70 years, you will have to go through that process.

When people want to get out of the process, and want the end results of the process, it gives birth to frustrations. When frustrations set in then they start taking shortcuts.

Anyone who has walked with God knows well that God does not do shortcuts. God watched His own Son go through process until the fullness of His time emanated. Jesus did not resurrect from the dead the day following His crucifixion.

There is a process for everything and every position. If you want to be a great Pastor, there is a process. If you want to be a Bishop, there is a process. God holds the times and seasons of process. When you go through the process some things may not go your way. It may seem like you failed at something. However, failure is an opinion. Your response to what happens while you are going through the process makes a difference.

Your perception is more important than the opinions of others. When you understand process, you will trust God to be victorious against what others may see as failure, but you know as valid progression.

CHAPTER 10: DON'T WALK IN THE SPIRIT OF ABSALOM

"Now I say, That the heir, as long as he is a child, differeth nothing from a servant, though he be lord of all; ² But is under tutors and governors until the time appointed of the father." (Gal 4:1-2)

WHO IS YOUR FATHER?

Can you trace the beginning of your Christian life? Who led you to Christ to be born again? What relationship did you have with that individual after being born again? Since you became born again, can you identify any mature Christian you submitted yourself to and learned at his feet the ways of God? If you are called to ministry, who has been grooming you for ministry?

If you struggle to answer the questions above, you may need to reflect over your Christian life. It is common for people to pride in the statement that they are "self-made". They may say that with a little pride; yet, most of the time people who claim to be self-made encounter problems later in their life. When they reach that stage, it is difficult to submit to someone for support.

The passage above makes it plain that being under the tutelage of a father is scriptural. Anyone who goes through the process of tutelage as a young growing person usually reaps the full benefits of his inheritance as an heir. Anyone who does not go through that process will have challenges in his Christian life and ministry. That is, if he feels called to serve in that capacity. Everyone needs a father figure in his life.

Fatherhood is an eternal principle that cannot be avoided. There are too many examples in biblical history to establish the fatherhood principle. Think of Moses and Joshua, of Elijah and Elisha, of Paul and Timothy, just to mention a few. Note that in these examples cited, the sons who stayed under the tutelage of their designated fathers until the fullness of their time accomplished great things, sometimes greater than their fathers achieved.

Fatherhood is a process involving an individual, a mature person who provides Godly counsel and guidance and support out of relevant experience, to another who is beginning life in any form, who submits to this mature individual who has gone ahead of him, through whom he learns the ways of whatever he is engaged in, for as long as God would like the process to last.

Even our Lord Jesus says that if we abide in Him and submit to His lordship and authority, we shall do greater things than He did. There is no substitute to fatherhood in life in general, and in ministry in particular.

The challenge today is that there are too many Christians in the body who have difficulty recognizing their spiritual father. The reason is simple. They have not grown under the tutelage of a mature, more experienced Christian, who has demonstrated knowledge of God over the years.

The possible causes are many. Sometimes such individuals do not want to be under authority as they grow in their Christian life. They cannot handle the discipline of learning under someone else. There are some who intentionally refuse to submit to anyone's leadership. There are some who believe they are self-made and owe no allegiance to anyone.

It is interesting, however, that many such individuals demand that others look up to them as spiritual fathers, the very thing they refused. Spiritually, that's not how it works.

> **It is an undeniable truth that cannot be contested anywhere, that if you have not**

> been properly fathered, you cannot father anyone. Better still, you may not have the moral authority to father anyone.

Very often people who have refused to be fathered by anyone mistake some things as evidence of spirituality: the gifts they manifest; or the amount of wealth they have accumulated either in their ministry, in their personal life, or both.

> It is totally wrong and unscriptural for anyone to equate anointing, gifts and talents, prosperity and wealth, or fame, to spirituality. In actual fact, you need to be spiritual to be able to function effectively under the anointing. If all you are is defined by how much money you have or how popular you have become, then you are most pitiful.

Too many up-and-coming pastors are in a hurry to have their names on billboards, or talk about their radio or TV ministries. Too many have taken titles upon themselves when there is little trace of evidence of Christian maturity.

One of the most common errors I have seen happening in the body today is the mistake of taking the gift of prophecy to mean operating in the office of the

Prophet. The result is that there are too many parading today as prophets, who do not have the calling into the office of the Prophet.

After several years of learning at the feet of Jesus, it is my desire that no one goes through the Christian life feeling he does not need to be fathered. Neither do I want to see people die spiritually or prematurely because they rebelled against their fathers instead of submitting and getting weaned when the appropriate time comes.

I want you to understand that you will never live under your father forever. You will eventually leave, so you do yourself a lot of good if you wait patiently under a spiritual father. There is nothing compared to leaving your father's house with his full blessing. Absalom, David's son, learned this the hard way. In fact, he did not even live to have the experience.

ABSALOM WAS A REBELLIOUS CHILD

Among his children, King David seemed to love Absalom the most. It is not wrong if anyone projects that it was the king's intention to groom him to reign after him as King of Israel. The problem with Absalom was that he wanted to avoid the process that would eventually get him the throne. He wanted to be king even when his father was still alive. He wanted to be recognized immediately.

He probably did not reckon with the fact that his father had to go through a process to become king. He did not want to prove himself in little things until it became obvious that he had what it took to be the next king.

Unfortunately for Absalom, we are talking about him, not like Job or even his father David, but as an example we should not follow. That's too bad for him.

THE SPIRIT OF ABSALOM

If you want to understand how the spirit of Absalom starts in an individual and how it operates in any system, read 2 Sam 15:1-31.

Absalom spent time with people who were going through challenges, which is a positive thing to do. The problem, however, was that his motive was wrong. Absalom just wanted to be made a judge. He was depicting himself as better than the leaders who had wisdom. That was the beginning of breeding disloyalty.

In the process he won the hearts of many and had some people following him. Absalom became a disloyal child who went behind his father. The king was not aware of it, neither did the leaders know about what was going on. With time, he had followers. "For the people increased continually with Absalom" (2 Sam 15:12).

Can your leader travel and leave the church for you to handle in his absence, being assured that by the time he returns, the church has not become yours with a new name and a new location? An Absalom spirit manifests in opportunism and self-advancement at the expense of others (2 Sam 15:2). When you started feeling that you could do some things better than your leader, what did you do with that feeling, knowing very well that you are not the one God has put in charge of the ministry?

What did you do with those feelings of frustration and pettiness over little things? What about finding fault with everything the leader does, the people he put in leadership, decisions he made about church finances, etc.?

An Absalom Spirit is rooted in a basic distrust and resentment of one's authority (2 Sam 13:20-21). It graduates into the spirit of independence. The clear manifestation of this is that the individual refuses to submit to the leader. Instead, he will apply manipulative tactics to get recognition of the followers. That was exactly what Absalom did.

The Absalom spirit manifests in impressing and stealing the hearts of the people who are under authority in order to eventually "dethrone" and replace the leader under whom you are supposed to be serving (2 Sam 15:1-12). For several years Absalom gradually took people's heart from his father. He had 200 men who accompanied him from Jerusalem. These people did not know his hidden agenda to take the throne from his father.

The Absalom spirit is the spirit of pride (2 Sam 14:23-26). With time, the individual gains recognition of the people and that is where pride sets in. When they heap praises upon him, he also believes that he is above everyone else.

The Absalom spirit comes out of hidden contempt, hidden hatred, and hidden revenge of authority and those under that authority (2 Sam 13:22). At what point did you find yourself questioning every decision your leader made, challenging every statement he made, and recommending your alternatives? What did you believe God was telling you to do?

When was it that you started gossiping about the leader, openly criticizing him, and making people feel that you could do better than he was doing? Now you are engrossed in open disloyalty and have become one who is operating a divisive spirit.

The Absalom spirit shows in hidden agendas, hidden strategies, and hidden alliances (2 Sam 13:22-29). Have you started holding secret meetings or discussing issues you have no business talking about?

People who walk in the Absalom spirit do not last. Very sadly, their end is pitiful. See how Absalom died. Absalom died because his glorious long hair got entangled in branches of a tree. His pride in lifting up his head over David's eventually killed him. He rode a mule and got caught under the thick boughs of a tree. The chariot left him, and he hung on his hair and was eventually killed (2 Sam 18:9-10).

You may not physically die like Absalom did, but if the Absalom spirit consumes you, your ministry will not last because whatever you sowed while under authority you will reap when you become the one in authority.

I cannot emphasize enough the role of a "Father", mentor, and tutor who have the maturity and have gone through their process and have been tested. Do not lean on the untested and the unprocessed; they will blind you and cause you to "charge God" foolishly.

AVOID THESE KILLERS

Make sure you handle the following in the most appropriate manner:

1. When you see another pastor or teacher or someone operating the office of a Prophet, or exhibiting any of the spiritual gifts, never be in a hurry to operate the same. That is not the time to go to God asking Him to give you that gift or get you into that office. Sometimes people push themselves hard and eventually go ahead of God because God does not violate process. That is the Absalom spirit. It is a way people get entangled in all kinds of spirits and some start practicing occultism.
2. When you see a pastor leading a 1500-member congregation, it is not an opportunity to also do things that will bring people to your church quickly so you can have those numbers in your congregation and show that you are also capable. That, too, is an Absalom spirit. Remember that God gives capacity to handle congregations of 50, 100, 300, 500, and 1,000 and in other multiples. If God has not given you that capacity yet, don't

force yourself into that category. When God gets you there, you will not struggle. God will bring the numbers and the grace to handle the numbers.

3. When you are serving under a seasoned pastor and your gift and calling begin to manifest, that is not the time to start having conflicts with your superior with the conclusion that God is leading you to start your own ministry. That is the Absalom spirit. Most people who do that are actually trying to bypass the process. It does not keep long for them to start experiencing untold hardship and challenges. You may leave and start "your own" ministry and it will take you years before you make a simple impact. If you don't receive special grace from God, you may never be heard of again.

4. The Bible teaches that as a child of God you can do all things through Christ who strengthens you. We know, however, that not everyone can do everything. The same God who inspired Paul to write that verse wrote that He has made some prophets, some teachers, some evangelists, after which there are gifts of administrations, etc., in the body. Some are empowered to some things and others are empowered to do different things. When you go through the process, you will not miss your true calling and the gift that enables you to function in your calling. Don't avoid the process.

5. Don't try to speak like the man of God you consider your role model. Speak like you and act like you because you may not have gone through what makes him speak and act the way he does.

Going through the process certainly helps you identify your true calling and the path destined for you to grow and become the great man of God you were meant to be.

Chapter 11: Don't Fight the Process

Embracing Every Bit of the Process

I would like to conclude this book with what is on my heart for up-and-coming Christians, particularly those who have a call to serve in God's vineyard. Whatever you do, never fight the process! God does not bypass the process.

As humans we fight and struggle against change and anything we do not understand. We resist process because we do not have all the answers. We ask many questions: *"How long will I go through it? Why do I have to go through it? What is for me at the end of the process?"*

> **Life is a process, so do not resist it and do not fight against it. Process and preparation will determine who you become and what you become.**

Go through the process. You are being prepared for something good. "But as it is written, eye hath not seen, nor ear heard, neither have entered into the heart of man, the things which God hath prepared for them that love him" (1 Cor 2:9). When you patiently go through the process, you will receive all the good God has in store for you.

God does not rush to bring you into His plans and purposes for your life. Remember God saying to the children of Israel that He would give them the land little by little:

> "I will send my fear before thee, and will destroy all the people to whom thou shalt come, and I will make all thine enemies turn their backs unto thee. And I will send hornets before thee, which shall drive out the Hivite, the Canaanite, and the Hittite, from before thee. I will not drive them out from before thee in one year; lest the land become desolate, and the beast of the field multiply against thee. By little and little I will drive them out from before thee, until thou be increased, and inherit the land." (Exo 23:27-30)

Little by little is God's process to bring you into full inheritance of what He has planned for you. If you want to avoid the process and have everything now, you place yourself in harm's way because when you are looking for God in your ways you will not find Him. You will find Him only in His ways.

You have to understand that even miracles are not acts that violate process. God works miracles when, in His sovereign will, the time is appropriate to do so. He generally works through the processes He Himself set in place.

JESUS CHRIST DID NOT FIGHT THE PROCESS

Jesus was born into a Jewish family. According to the custom of the Jews, a man must attain a certain age before you receive recognition as one who can engage in activities in the open place. Jesus had to wait to attain that age. Is it possible He could have started performing miracles at an earlier age, like 12? Absolutely, yes! Remember at age 12 he was already asking the Scribes and Pharisees questions for which they had no answers. When his parents looked for Him and finally found him, listen carefully to the answer he gave them, "Didn't you know that I must be about my Father's business" (Luke 2:49).

His father's business included preaching, teaching, casting out devils, healing, performing miracles, and eventually dying to save humanity. Who would listen to a 12-year old if he says he had come to save people from their sins? Jesus had to wait and even get baptized to fulfill all Jewish righteousness.

Why can't we follow the example of Jesus instead of wanting everything happening overnight like the magicians do?

> God can perform miracles every day, anywhere, and at anytime. When it comes to sharing a platform with Him in ministry on a consistent basis for a long time, no man can skip the process of preparation.

Violating this principle amounts to fighting the process. There are a few elements of process that you do not have to bypass. I am discussing a few of them here:

DISCIPLESHIP [MENTORING] IS CRITICAL

"Now I say that the heir, as long as he is a child does not differ at all from a slave, though he is master of all, but is under guardians and stewards until the time appointed by the father" (Gal 4:1-2).

The Apostle Paul taught this principle in talking about our salvation; however, it actually is an eternal principle that is very true also about coming of age in your desire to serve in God's vineyard.

This principle is known today in most human development processes as mentoring. In mentoring, an inexperienced learner submits to a process by which he is guided through life by a more experienced person, especially in common fields of endeavor.

Mentoring is usually a process people go through in preparation for their intended vocation for life. For example, if you want to do business, you can have an experienced businessman as a mentor who will help you navigate the process of becoming successful. When you subject yourself to mentoring, you avoid making unnecessary mistakes and save yourself the trouble of going through some unwarranted situations. God uses your mentor to shape your life to conform to His standards and expectations.

You have to understand that mentoring is not a man-made principle. It is a God-ordained principle. It has its roots in Deuteronomy 6, when God commanded the Israelites to teach their children His ways. It is echoed again in Proverbs 22:6, where the preacher wrote, "Train a child the way in which he should go and when he is grown, he will not depart from it".

Be patient and learn under an experienced servant of God. It will not kill your zeal. It will refine and smoothen the rough edges of your life.

ELIJAH AND ELISHA

Elijah and Elisha's relationship is a perfect example of discipleship and mentoring in the Old Testament. Elisha was humble enough to learn from his master up until the day he was taken to heaven in a chariot.

Elisha followed his master from Gilgal, to Bethel, to Jericho, and to Jordan. Though Elijah asked Elisha to stay in Gilgal, Elisha declined. He wanted to follow his master. He followed him until he came to Jordan. It was at that point he could ask for a double portion of his spirit, one of the very popular prayers that believers pray. Everyone today is going to God and asking for a double portion of His Spirit.

> The double portion you are asking of God will be given you when you are going through the process God Himself instituted for your preparation for fruitful service. If you skip the process, avoid it, or fight it, your prayers are not enough for you to receive a double portion.

The danger is that when people skip the process and therefore miss out on God's original, they settle for a counterfeit without knowing. The reason they do not know it is because they spent 60 days in prayer and fasting asking for a double portion so they conclude they have it.

If you study carefully the relationship between Elisha and Elijah, you will understand the process Elisha had to go through until the fullness of the time came.

Learn to Grow under Authority

Think of authority for a moment. When Jesus gave the disciples the Great Commission, He told them, "All authority in heaven and on earth has been given to me" (Matt 28:18). Study carefully His three-year relationship with the disciples and note that He transferred the same authority He had to them only after they had learned His ways, understood Him, and gone through personal transformation due to the discipleship process. They learned to be under Jesus' authority for a period of three and a half years. Then they learned what it takes to also operate under the authority of Jesus.

Note well also, that all the miracles they performed after Jesus had ascended to heaven were done under His authority. They learned they had to be under Jesus' authority before they could exercise authority over the powers of darkness. They could not cast out demons in their own names, but in the name of Jesus only! That is how authority works – you have to be under authority to exercise authority.

> **You must first learn to be under authority before you can have authority. If you are in a hurry to get to the top and skip the process of learning to stay under authority, you cannot be given authority.**

You may get to the top you have in mind, but your authority will be limited. You will never have learned the principles of authority so you are likely to abuse the authority you have received. The chances are that you will also have people under you who will also not recognize your authority. We do not need to perpetuate that spirit in the body of Christ today!

CHECK YOUR MOTIVES

People who don't want to go through the process take a single scripture and twist it to suit their motives. Take for example God's promise, "Ask what you will and My Father will do it" (John 14:13).

When we quote God saying, "He said we should ask and we shall receive", we have to put it in its proper context. Asking to receive itself is a process. The promises of God are not contained in a vacuum. They are intertwined in God's overall package.

Elsewhere in the Scriptures for example, you will encounter the truth that you must ask according to God's will. If you ask anything according to the will of God, you will have them.

Later on, you will learn from Apostle James that you ask and do not receive because you ask so you can consume it upon your lusts (Jam 4:3). That is where motive comes in. When you are in a hurry to get to the top, no matter how hard you pray, God knows you do not yet have what it takes to stay at the top and, therefore, will not answer such prayers.

When your prayers before God are aimed at feeding your ego, God knows it. He will not answer those prayers, according to the Apostle James.

> **God does not contradict Himself. The truth is that God's promises are packaged in systems and processes He has instituted, so the people who embrace the package are those who get the fullness of those promises.**

When you miss out on God, you create the platform for all the necromancy and all kinds of occultist activities, with people operating familiar spirits in the name of the Holy Spirit.

GUARD AGAINST COMPETITION

When you fight the process, you put yourself in competition with others when you are expected to work in collaboration with them. It is all because you want to get to the top quickly and compare yourself with another brother who, in your opinion, should not have been at the top. You think he is not being as spiritual as he can be.

Guard against competition that breeds covetousness. That is idolatry.

If we are all supposed to be in the same boat, heading to the same destination, called by the same Lord, operating generally the same, except each of us has some uniqueness, where is the place for competition? We are expected to grow together, "compacted by that which every joint supplies" (Eph 4:16).

The world's system promotes fierce competition. They sell it to us and we are gradually accepting it. Sometimes they call it "healthy competition". We always know that the human heart struggles to handle terms like that.

If, for example, a pastor stands in public to say his church is better than any other church around, what is healthy about such competition? When a believer looks at other believers and tells them, "I am the head here and not the tail", what is he trying to imply? Is that also supposed to be healthy competition?

When a pastor declares, "I am going to do something that no pastor has ever done in this country", what is that supposed to mean? All such statements charge the atmosphere with the spirit of competition and very soon we are comparing ourselves with each other in an unhealthy manner instead of collaborating.

> The problem with competition is that those who want to beat the competition and be ahead of everyone, become vulnerable and do not want to go through process. They often want shortcuts to the top and engage in anything fair or foul to get recognition.

Chapter 12: Wrestle for the Future

"And Jacob was left alone; and there wrestled a man with him until the breaking of the day. And when he saw that he prevailed not against him, he touched the hollow of his thigh; and the hollow of Jacob's thigh was out of joint, as he wrestled with him. And he said, Let me go, for the day breaketh. And he said, I will not let thee go, except thou bless me." (Gen 32:24-26)

There is a difference between a boxing fight and a wrestling match. In a boxing fight, the ideal objective is to knock out your opponent, knock him down to the count to ten, or win by scoring points. However, in a wrestling match all you need do is to keep a hold on the opponent, pinning him down until the count to three.

The passage above describes a unique experience Jacob had. In this experience, Jacob did not fight. The Bible says, "he wrestled" with what was in front of him. Sometimes we want to fight, we want to knock down and knock out the light of the process, when God wants us to hold on to the future and pin down our faith and trust in Him, holding on to His promises until the count is out.

THERE IS A BLESSING IN THE TUSSLE

Jacob was determined that no matter what scars or limps he would get during his process, he would not go through it without obtaining a blessing. He would not let go his wrestling process until it had released its intended blessing. In the midst of the process, Jacob kept his mind on the blessing. He understood and was unwavering in his conviction that what he was dealing with was not in vain.

> **Your life may be put out of joint during the wrestling process but, like Jacob, look for the blessing, and learn from the lesson of your wrestling process. Let the limp of the process be a memorial, a badge of honor, of a veteran of process, showcasing the blessing obtained and not the pain received during your process.**

Jacob's wrestling and his walk changed. He learned through the process to lean on the everlasting arm and not the hand of flesh.

REDEFINE YOURSELF

"And he said unto him, What is thy name? And he said, Jacob. And he said, Thy name shall be called no more Jacob, but Israel: for as a prince hast thou power with God and with men, and hast prevailed. And Jacob asked him, and said, Tell me, I pray thee, thy name. And he said, Wherefore is it that thou dost ask after my name? And he blessed him there."
(Gen 32:27-29)

Jacob was wrestling with something he could not see. It was night. Sometimes you cannot see, know, nor understand what is wrestling with you in life. It is all part of the process. But your process is a defining moment. Your attitude toward it will define your identity for what is ahead of you.

You can let the challenges of the process expose and highlight your weakness, helplessness, and past, in a way that disempowers you; or, you can see it as an opportunity to rebrand yourself and align your mindset with your destiny.

The angel used the process to help Jacob change his perspective about himself. His name was Jacob but his identity was Israel, one who had power with God!

Through the wrestling process, God matched and, thereby, changed the name of Jacob to Israel, to reflect how God saw him.

> **When you go through your process, you will discover that you are no longer what you used to be. God is sculpting and molding you through your process to fit the image He has of you, making you "meet" for your assignment.**

Focus on What is Being Changed in You

You help yourself a lot if you focus on what is being changed in you rather than on what is being used to change you. "And Jacob asked him, and said, Tell me, I pray thee, thy name. And he said, Wherefore is it that thou dost ask after my name? And he blessed him there" (Gen 32:29).

It is not what the process is called that is important. Others will label your process. They will have medical terms, financial status, social standing, legal frameworks, etc. You may be called desolate and forsaken. You may be stigmatized, branded, or defamed. These are all calculated to cause you to fight and resist the process, to succumb to shortcuts.

> **Don't be preoccupied with what men and circumstances try to pin on you. When you overcome they will change your name.**

Joseph could have been labeled a wishful thinker, a slave, a rapist, or a convict, but when he became prime minister, all that changed.

Don't be Mindful of Man's Labeling

At best, men's labeling of you will get you to circumvent the process. It is important therefore to guard against being so mindful of man's labeling.

> **Sometimes you have to be alone for God to have your undivided attention. Jacob had to separate himself from his wives and family to face his wrestling process alone.**

There are things written in the volume of the books that will never be revealed until God has your undivided attention. When God gets your undivided attention, you have no time to consider what labels men are putting on you.

Thank God that Jacob's wrestling with Him happened when there was no one around. The wrestling process brought out the original intent of God for his life.

Power with God and man is a product of wrestling with God. Wrestle for your future, instead of fighting the process. Wrestle in prayer until you get every answer you are expecting. Wrestle to hold on to your faith and convictions about God's specific intentions for your life.

Conclusion

I want to end by emphasizing the importance of teaching your kids about process. If you children do not learn about going through the process they will not endure in difficult times. Teach them to learn to wait for their turn, and also to know that all things don't come at the same time. Going through a process will prepare them for their whole life. Process ensures longevity. So, let them learn to wait on God to properly grow as spiritual people.

www.ingramcontent.com/pod-product-compliance
Lightning Source LLC
Chambersburg PA
CBHW031647040426
42453CB00006B/237